ARCHITECTURE

Eleanor Van Zandt

A Division of Steck-Vaughn Company
Austin, Texas

The Arts

Architecture
Dance
Design
Literature
The Movies
Music
Painting and Sculpture
Photography
Theater

Cover illustration: Sydney Opera House, Sydney, Australia

Series editor: Rosemary Ashley
Book editor: Clare Pumfrey
Designer: David Armitage
Consultant: Donald Smith
History of Architecture Department
South Bank Polytechnic, London

Published in the United States in 1990 by Steck-Vaughn Co. Austin, Texas, a subsidiary of National Education Corporation

First published in 1989 by Wayland (Publishers) Limited

©Copyright 1989 Wayland (Publishers) Ltd.

Library of Congress Cataloging-in-Publication Data

Van Zandt, Eleanor.
   Architecture / Eleanor Van Zandt.
     p. cm.—(The Arts)
   Includes bibliographical references.
   Summary: A general history and overview of architecture from the Egyptian pyramids to contemporary forms. Discusses Oriental, Islamic, and pre-Columbian architecture as well as European and later styles that developed in the United States.
   ISBN 0-8114-2362-X
   1. Architecture—Juvenile literature.   [1. Architecture.]
I. Title. II. Series: Arts (Austin, Tex.)
NA200.V36   1989   89-21973
720—dc20   CIP
                                                    AC

Typeset by Multifacit Graphics, Keyport, NJ
Printed in Italy by Rotolito
Bound in the United States
1 2 3 4 5 6 7 8 9 0 Ro 94 93 92 91 90

Contents

1 Architecture and Our Environment 4

2 The Ancient World 9

3 Exotic Forms 13

4 Castles and Cathedrals 18

5 A Sense of Proportion 23

6 Splendor and Elegance 28

7 Something Old, Something New 33

8 Modern Lines 37

9 Learning to Look at Architecture 42

Glossary 45

Further Reading 46

Index 47

1 Architecture and Our Environment

Of all the arts, architecture is the one that most directly affects people in their daily lives. Almost everyone in the developed world lives in a building of some sort and works, studies, and shops in other buildings. Almost every event or activity in which we take part—going to a movie, a sports event, or a party; going on vacation; getting married; staying in a hospital—derives some of its character from the surroundings in which it takes place.

In the long term, people can be affected quite seriously by their architectural environment. After World War II (1939–45) the new trend in public housing was for people to live in bleak apartment buildings surrounded by empty stretches of grass. This has proved to be a social—as well as aesthetic—disaster. The original sense of community disintegrated in these anonymous vertical "egg boxes." Deprived of the sociability of a neighborhood street and of a sense of individuality, people withdraw into their own little worlds. Depression, alcoholism, and vandalism are some of the by-products.

Of course, bad architecture cannot be blamed for all our social ills, although sometimes it must seem to architects that they are the universal scapegoats. But there is a growing recognition by the public that how and what we build is important. We all have a responsibility for the appearance of our environment and a right to insist, first, that the good buildings erected by previous generations not be wantonly destroyed and, second, that what we erect beside them—however different that may be—should be of as high a standard as possible. All of us can become more aware of our surroundings, and more visually sophisticated, and learn to take an active part in the development of our environment.

Quite apart from any practical usefulness it may have, a basic knowledge and appreciation of architecture can make a vacation or a stroll through our own town or village more interesting and more rewarding—in the same way that knowing the names of plants and animals makes a walk in the countryside more enjoyable.

In the following pages we shall look at some of the many styles of building all over the world created throughout history, and at some of the great architectural masterpieces. We shall also discover some of the ideas behind the planning and design of these buildings. First, however, we need to look briefly at a few of the essentials—both practical and aesthetic—used by architects of all times and places.

The two basic components of architecture are space and mass. Of the two, mass is the more obvious. When we look at any building from the outside, we can see its shape, or mass, immediately. We notice whether

Below *This grim apartment building in southeast London is typical of much postwar public housing. The crude graffiti scrawled on the wall may well reflect the residents' response to their environment.*

Below *A close-up view of the colonnade surrounding St. Peter's Square in Rome shows the mastery of its architect, Gianlorenzo Bernini (1598–1680), in handling the elements of mass and space. From the center of this vast square, or piazza, one has little idea of the massiveness of the columns.*

the different parts that together form the whole building are tall or low, curved or straight, symmetrical or asymmetrical. Then, when we go inside a building, we experience the space or spaces enclosed by its external and internal frames. The quality of this experience determines to a great extent the quality of the architecture.

The relationship between mass and space varies enormously from building to building. The pyramids of ancient Egypt, for example, represent an architecture of almost pure mass. They are pierced with chambers and passageways, but from outside they look like solid, geometrically regular piles of masonry. At the other extreme, the colonnade enclosing St. Peter's Square, in Rome, is primarily an architecture of space. The columns themselves are massive, but they are arranged in great curving arms, intended to suggest the embracing of the faithful by the Mother Church; and when the square is full of pilgrims, that is exactly what they do.

In most buildings the elements of mass and space are in a more balanced, if complex, relationship than in an Egyptian pyramid or St. Peter's Square. In a Gothic cathedral, for example, we are aware of the soaring height in the nave and the great distance from the west end to the high altar. But at the same time we see that this space is shaped and subdivided by other structures, such as the great piers made up of slender stone columns that fan out as they rise to form the ribs of the vault. There may also be a row of arches with galleries above, and all sorts of intricately carved shapes projecting from the main structure. As we walk through the building, both the spaces and the solid shapes seem to change, and new relationships become apparent. Thus we discover one of the most fascinating aspects of architecture: that within the essential stability of a building, we can experience change and movement.

Gothic architecture represents a beautiful solution to the architect's most basic problem: how to cover a space in a way that will withstand the pull of gravity. The physical and mathematical factors that an architect has to consider in planning a building are much too complex to discuss here; but a general idea of the various ways in which this fundamental problem can be solved will help us to appreciate the changes in style that have occurred throughout history, and how architects of the past (and of today) have made use of new technology.

The walls of a building may be either load-bearing—that is, supporting the roof and floors and everything standing on them—or non-load-bearing. A solid wall of stone, brick, or concrete will carry quite a heavy load, although, in general, the farther apart the walls are, the lighter the load must be. In contrast, a non-load-bearing wall is a skeletal structure consisting of a frame that carries the weight, covered or filled in with material of a lighter weight. A medieval half-timbered cottage and a modern steel and glass skyscraper both have non-load-bearing walls.

The space between the walls may be spanned by straight beams or by a curved structure, such as an arch, vault, or dome. A straight beam supported at both ends is called a post-and-lintel, or trabeated, construction. It is simpler to build than an arch—every child who plays with blocks discovers it—but an arch can span much greater distances. This is because the pull of gravity is more evenly distributed in an arch and so no part of the structure is under extreme stress. In both types of construction, the weight may be carried by walls or columns, or by a combination of the two. The roof of a building may be supported by a structure called a truss. This is a series of triangular frames that are self-supporting and carry the weight of the roof.

There is a close relationship between the way a building is constructed and the materials used. For example, in densely populated parts of the United States, where timber is plentiful and accessible, most houses have timber frames. In countries where timber is now relatively scarce, load-bearing walls of stone or brick are more commonly seen. Before the innovations of the twentieth century, most

Right *The interior of King's College Chapel, Cambridge (1508–15) perfectly illustrates the feeling of spaciousness, created partly by the height of the vaulted ceilings, inside a great Gothic church. The fan vaulting, seen here over the nave, is a distinguishing feature of the last phase of English Gothic, called Perpendicular.*

Inset *The Seagram Building, in New York (1958), designed by Mies van der Rohe and Philip Johnson, has a skeletal steel frame and walls of glass. The bronze-colored glass lends some richness to the elegantly severe design.*

important buildings were built in stone—at least their walls were—not only because of its durability but because it can be finished in so many ways: cut roughly to suggest the quarry itself or smoothed into blocks known as ashlar, for a refined appearance; carved in relief or in delicate tracery for a window; or, in the case of marble, polished to bring out beautiful colors and patterns.

Inset *These gracious seventeenth-century houses, with their mellow colors, are typical of old Amsterdam.*

Below *Whitewashed houses on the Greek island of Santorini contrast dramatically with the blue sea and sky. The white walls reflect the heat, and the small windows keep out the sunlight, making the houses cool havens during the hot weather.*

The sensuous qualities of stone and other materials greatly affect the visual impact made by a building. The glistening white stucco of Greek houses against a lapis lazuli blue sky, the mellow golden stone of an English farmhouse, or the crisp contrast of dark red brick and white window frames in a Georgian townhouse are only a few of the pleasures of texture and color to be enjoyed by anyone who keeps their eyes open and observes.

Indeed, one of the most often criticized aspects of twentieth-century architecture has been its lack of sensuous appeal. The structural possibilities and relative cheapness of such materials as prestressed concrete and plate glass appear, to some people, to have contributed to an architecture that does little to engage the senses and, in some cases, positively repels them. Inevitably, economics play a major part in the choice of materials, but there are usually possibilities for enlivening the surface of a building in some inexpensive way. Recently there has been a return to the use of more colorful materials, in a clear effort to restore to our towns and cities some of the visual richness they have lost.

2 The Ancient World

The wealth of materials and techniques available to modern architects could not have been imagined by the people who created the first great architecture, some 6,000 years ago, in Mesopotamia. Early civilizations inhabited the region between the Tigris and Euphrates rivers, now part of Iraq. Here, complex societies developed, with economies able to support the building of cities. Architecture—apart from the most basic forms of shelter—is a product of a wealthy and highly structured society, with institutions, such as a government and an organized religion, that create the demand for important buildings. Other arts, such as music, painting, or dance, can develop in much simpler societies.

In Mesopotamia by about 4000 B.C. one civilization after another—the Sumerian city-states, then the Babylonian and Assyrian empires—flourished. These structured societies built great cities, dominated by imposing buildings, such as fortifications, palace complexes, and stepped pyramids. The pyramids were called ziggurats, and were crowned by a temple in which a god was believed to dwell. One such ziggurat may have been the Tower of Babel, mentioned in the Bible. Another famous example of Babylonian architecture was the terraced Hanging Gardens built by King Nebuchadnezzar.

Unfortunately, little remains of ancient Mesopotamian architecture, because it was built mainly of mud bricks, originally sundried, later baked, as there was little stone in this region. The mud bricks have since crumbled away. In Egypt, however, stone was plentiful. The ancient Egyptians built their massive temples and pyramids of granite, many of which survive today.

Above *The pyramids of kings Cheops, Chephren, and Mycerinus, at Giza are among the oldest surviving structures in the world, dating from about 2500 B.C. The largest pyramid is 450 feet high, and contains about 2,300,000 blocks of limestone. The pyramids were apparently intended as tombs, in which the mummified kings were buried with their valued possessions. The Egyptians believed that these would accompany them to the afterlife.*

Above *The Parthenon stands imposingly above the city of Athens. Its grandeur is emphasized by the eight Doric columns across the entrance front, instead of the more usual six.*

Inset *The temple of Sobek, the Egyptian crocodile god, at Kom Ombo in Upper Egypt.*

Although much Egyptian architecture is richly decorated with paintings and carved designs, such as palm leaves and lotus blossoms, it still looks very solid and imposing. This effect is not achieved merely by the size of the buildings; it results also from giving them gently sloping, or battered, sides, in order to make them resistant to earthquakes. The smooth, massive columns that supported the roofs of temples, although often carved to suggest bundles of papyrus reeds, have a similarly heavy, solid look.

It was the Greeks who brought the column to its highest degree of perfection and so created the most enduring motif in Western architecture. Rows of Greek-inspired columns are so familiar a part of our architectural landscape that we seldom think of their origin or look at them closely. They are found on churches, courthouses, university buildings, banks, hotels, and houses. They are used today, as they have been since the Renaissance, to give a building an aura of seriousness and to link it symbolically with a host of ideas—political, philosophical, and artistic—derived from the Greek and Roman civilizations. We call the architecture of ancient Greece and Rome (which adapted Greek styles) Classical. The style is characterized by dignity, restraint, and a combination of exact proportions.

Columns are the most distinctive feature of Classical architecture. They were used primarily to support the roofs of temples, by far the most important type of building in ancient Greece. In the earliest temples, the columns were made of timber. Later temples, built of limestone or marble and embellished with sculpture, were built using the original simple post-and-lintel method of construction. One of the most satisfying aspects of Greek architecture is this fusion of elegant style with a simple structure.

Over the course of several centuries the Greeks developed three distinct styles, or orders, of column—the Doric, the Ionic, and the Corinthian. The Romans developed two other styles—Roman Doric and Composite. The Doric was the earliest and consisted of a tapering shaft, rising directly from the floor, topped with a plain, cushionlike capital. The Roman Doric column has a base, unlike the Greek Doric column that appears to grow straight out of the ground. The later orders are more elegant, more slender in relation to their height, and crowned with capitals gracefully carved to suggest scrolls or foliage.

The masterpiece of Classical Greek architecture, the Parthenon, was built in the Doric style. Situated on the Acropolis, overlooking Athens, this temple was dedicated to the city's patron goddess, Athena, and originally housed a gigantic statue of her. Like all Greek temples, it was thought of as the deity's dwelling place, not as a house of worship. Religious rituals were conducted in front of the temple—one reason for the emphasis given to the exteriors of these buildings.

Today the Parthenon is a ruin, and most of the beautiful sculpture that adorned it is in the British Museum in London. But enough remains of the building to illustrate the Greeks' mastery of harmonious proportions. Close study of the building has also revealed that its

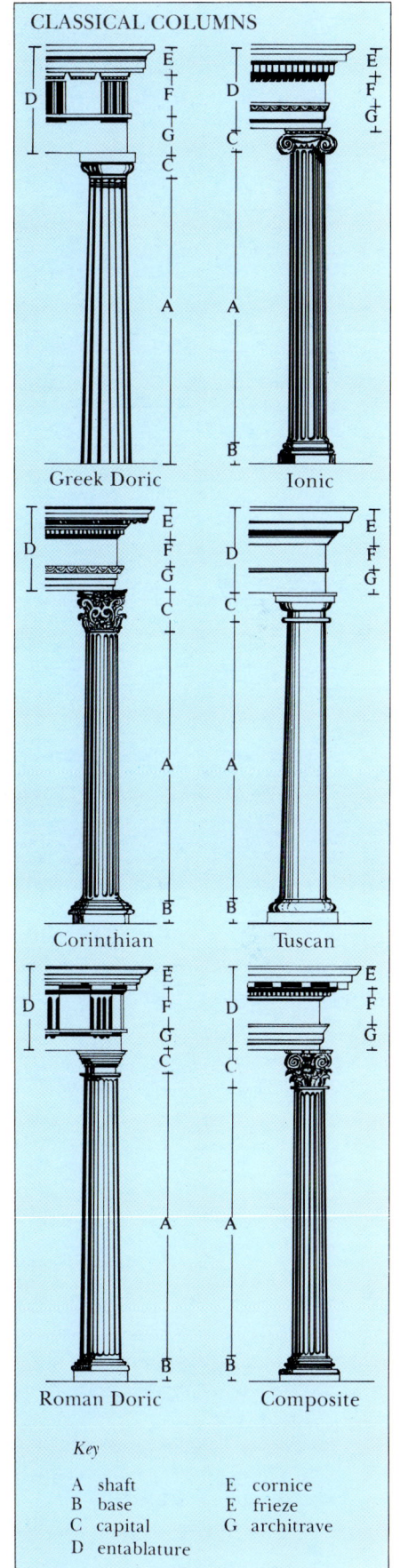

CLASSICAL COLUMNS

Greek Doric   Ionic

Corinthian   Tuscan

Roman Doric   Composite

Key

A shaft
B base
C capital
D entablature
E cornice
F frieze
G architrave

11

Above *The Pantheon, Rome. The coffered interior of the dome, made of concrete, was originally gilded. The building was designed on two identical circles, one horizontal, one vertical; so the diameter of the dome equals the distance from the oculus to the floor.*

perfection is partly the result of an extremely subtle use of optical illusion. It appears to be composed of straight lines, but in fact there is scarcely a right angle in it. The Greeks discovered that if the long horizontal lines of the temple were straight in reality, they would look as if they were bending and sagging. So, to correct this optical illusion, both the stylobate (platform) on which the columns stand and the entablature (horizontal beam) they support curve upward by about 2.3 inches in the middle. Similarly, the columns are not of an even width from top to bottom but swell very slightly in the middle and taper toward the top of the shaft. This swelling, called *entasis*, prevents them from appearing concave. They also slant inward slightly, and those at the corners are a little closer to and larger than their neighbors, to prevent them from looking thinner than the others as they are silhouetted against the sky. Some of these optical refinements were used in other Classical buildings, but nowhere are they employed to such superb effect as in the Parthenon.

The importance of public life to the Greeks can be seen in their city planning. The *agora*, for instance, was a marketplace in the center of the city, lined with covered colonnades, where citizens could stroll or sit and talk, sheltered from the glare of the Mediterranean sun. Another important aspect of Greek life was the theater. Many huge amphitheaters were built on the hillsides outside Greek cities.

The Romans also built temples, theaters, and their equivalent of the *agora*, the *forum*. But they also developed other types of building to suit their own way of life and the needs of the Empire: multistory apartment houses called *insulae*; great rectangular meeting halls called basilicas; aqueducts; arenas; and triumphal arches, through which their victorious armies marched.

Although the Romans did not invent the arch, they exploited it with great skill. This method of construction, along with their development of various kinds of concrete, allowed them to create an architecture capable of spanning wider areas, one that depended less upon columns and more upon walls.

The typically Roman combination of Greek styles and their own structural ingenuity can be seen in the Colosseum in Rome. Here the three Greek orders are used on the exterior walls, one above the other, in the form of attached columns whose purpose is decorative rather than functional. A complex system of arches and tunnels, some visible and some concealed, supports the building.

Another magnificent building in Rome, the Pantheon (the temple of all the gods), illustrates the Romans' mastery of the dome. Behind an imposing portico, the walls of this drum-shaped building consist of layers of brick-faced concrete. They support a vast semicircular concrete dome, originally faced with gilded bronze, measuring 142 feet in diameter. The dome is pierced with a 28-foot circular opening, called an oculus, which floods the interior with light. Still remarkably well preserved today, nearly 1,900 years after it was built, the Pantheon is an impressive tribute to Roman architecture.

3 Exotic Forms

After Rome fell to barbarian invaders in the fifth century A.D. and the western part of the Empire disintegrated, very little building on a large scale took place in Europe until the beginning of the eleventh century. However, the eastern part of the Empire remained—it was governed from Constantinople (formerly Byzantium, today Istanbul). Here, under the patronage of Christian emperors, a new kind of religious architecture began to evolve.

One of the outstanding features of this Byzantine architecture was the development of the dome. Eastern Orthodox churches are usually

Left *The interior of the Church of St. Sophia, Istanbul (formerly Constantinople), showing one of the semicircular apses flanking the central domed space. The Islamic script, pulpit (right), and enclosed gallery for women (left) date from the time when the church was used as a mosque.*

Above *The elaborate tile work on this portal in the mosque of Masjid-i-Shah, Isfahan, Iran, shows the Islamic genius for intricate pattern. The wide, pointed arch is another characteristic of Islamic architecture.*

centrally planned, often in the form of a Greek cross, unlike Western churches, which usually have a Latin cross, or elongated, plan. The center of the Greek cross was emphasized by crowning it with a dome. Byzantine architects developed this feature with breathtaking skill. Instead of supporting the dome on a cylindrical base, as the Romans had done, they succeeded in placing it over a square space—a much more difficult feat. In order to do this, curved supports, called pendentives, were built from the corners of the square to the base of the dome. The pendentives direct the weight of the dome down into the supporting columns at the corners of the square.

This method of construction enabled architects to open out the walls around the central space and build hemispherical domes above them. This was achieved most brilliantly in the great Church of St. Sophia, in Constantinople, completed in A.D. 537. In this astonishing building, one great domed space seems to grow out of another. Walls and domes are pierced with arches, galleries, and many windows, producing a mysterious interplay of light and shadow. Later Greek Orthodox churches tended to have darker interiors, but here, too, a sense of awe and sanctity is created by the flicker of candlelight upon the gold of the mosaics and icons.

Variations on the Byzantine style of architecture were developed wherever Orthodox Christianity was established. In Russia, for example, churches sprout clusters of onion-shaped domes, which are often gilded on the outside or carved and painted in fantastic designs. The dome-shaped roofs also have a practical advantage in northern climates because they do not collect snow.

Domes are also a prominent feature of Islamic architecture. The religion of Islam was born in Arabia in the seventh century A.D. Over the next few centuries it spread throughout the Middle East and North Africa, then into Spain and southern Asia, as far as India. Although the architecture of these far-flung parts of the Islamic world has many regional variations, it reflects, in varying degrees, the desert origins of Islam, the hot climates in which it flourished, and, of course, its teachings.

Most Islamic palaces and mosques are built around one or more courtyards, usually containing fountains. They are the architectural equivalents of the oasis—so vital to the desert nomads. In Arabia and North Africa especially, the exterior of these buildings is comparatively plain. This is an inward-looking architecture. The courtyards are often surrounded by covered arcades, providing welcome shade from the hot sun. The openness of the plan, with rooms, arcades, and courtyards flowing into one another, provides maximum ventilation, and the splashing of the fountains not only creates an impression of coolness, but also provides it.

Both mosques and palaces share these features, but the mosque is easily distinguished from the outside by its slender towers, called minarets. It is from the top of a minaret that the muezzin calls the faithful to prayer.

Islam forbids the representation of living beings in religious art, and so Islamic artists have traditionally directed their talents toward creating intricate abstract decoration. Walls, domes, and minarets are richly adorned with patterned tiles, mosaics, and stone filigree and with beautiful calligraphy, in the form of quotations from the Koran, the Muslim holy book. Blue, green, and turquoise are the colors most often used.

The most famous example of Islamic architecture, the Taj Mahal at Agra in India, is neither a mosque nor a palace but a mausoleum. It was built in the mid-seventeenth century by the Indian emperor Shah Jehan, for his favorite wife. Its perfectly harmonious grouping of domes and arches, faced with radiant white marble, inlaid in patterns and delicately carved to suggest lace, make it an eloquent declaration of love. As if to repeat this declaration again and again, the building is reflected in the surface of four canals that lead away from each façade. Four tapering minarets flank the tomb, at a respectful distance, like sentinels.

In striking contrast to the abstract decoration of Islamic architecture, Hindu temples are lavishly encrusted with figurative sculpture, depicting gods and goddesses, dancers and animals, with astonishing vitality. The shrine of the temple, where the god is believed to dwell, is topped by the *sikhara*, a hollow conical or pyramid-shaped structure symbolizing a mountain. The worshipers enter a series of courtyards or vestibules around the shrine.

Below *The Taj Mahal, at Agra, India. Faced with white marble, this is considered by many people to be the most beautiful building in the world. It was designed as the focus of a series of riverside gardens. The four slender towers are minarets. Open vaulted halls, known as* iwans, *lead from the outside to the central chamber, above which rises the great dome.*

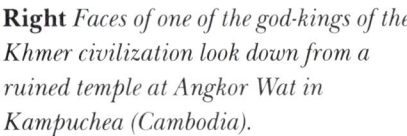

Right *Faces of one of the god-kings of the Khmer civilization look down from a ruined temple at Angkor Wat in Kampuchea (Cambodia).*

Below *The Temple of Heaven (1420), Beijing. This building, with its complex tiered roof (a feature of pagodas, also) and its use of rich colors, especially red, is typical of Chinese architecture. Color plays an important part in Chinese architecture. The greatest variety of painted decoration is found on palace buildings.*

The Hindu idea of the temple as an image of the Cosmos is most dramatically expressed in the vast temple complex of Angkor Wat, in Kampuchea. It was built by the Khmer civilization in the twelfth century as a sanctuary for the god Vishnu and as a mortuary temple. This rectangular structure is enclosed by a wall 10 miles long and by a moat that was intended to represent the ocean and once formed part of an extensive irrigation system. At the center of the complex is the temple itself, reached by a series of steep terraces. It is an elaborate stepped pyramid, crowned by five lotus towers, which symbolizes Mount Meru, the center of the Universe.

The civilization of China has traditionally placed less emphasis on architecture than on other fine arts, such as painting, so there are few examples of monumental architecture in that country. This is also a result of the Chinese preference for building in wood or brick, relatively perishable materials compared with stone. However, Chinese buildings are ingeniously built. Their most distinctive feature is the roof, which normally curves upward and overhangs the main structure. These graceful roofs are supported by a complex rectangular system of beams and by clusters of brackets called *koutung*.

The most characteristic Chinese building, the pagoda, shows the fascination with roof construction; each story of the pagoda is capped with wide, curving eaves. Originally, pagodas were religious buildings, constructed in stone or brick, which is why so many have survived when contemporary wooden buildings have disappeared. Later pagodas were monuments to victory or symbols of good luck.

In architecture, as in so many other arts, the Japanese drew on Chinese models. However, they showed more interest in exploring the potential of these buildings, as can be seen in the splendid Japanese pagodas, with their very wide eaves, and the exuberant, many-gabled castles perched high above the towns.

Unlike the Chinese, the Japanese have a preference for asymmetry. This characteristic is one of the hallmarks of the Japanese house, and has had an enormous influence on many twentieth-century Western architects. Its two other notable characteristics are simplicity and flexibility. The houses are usually one-story with a timber frame because of the frequency of earthquakes in Japan. The lightweight interior walls are supplemented by sliding paper screens, used to partition rooms as required. Furniture is almost nonexistent, but the quality of the materials used, the careful display of a few beautiful objects and, in warm weather, the unrestricted view of a serene garden make the Japanese house restful and inviting.

Before the first contact with European explorers in the fifteenth century, the peoples of the American continents developed their cultures and societies in isolation. The evidence of their sophisticated skills in architecture remains today.

When the Spanish conquistadors reached the Aztec capital of Tenochtitlán, in Mexico, they found it an impressive city built of stone and dominated by several stepped pyramids. Tenochtitlán was razed by the conquerors and rebuilt as Mexico City; but other stepped pyramids can be found elsewhere in Mexico. Those of the Mayan civilization are especially distinctive, with their steep sides, decorated with sculpture and other details. Like Aztec pyramids, they have wide stairways, leading up to a small temple, in front of which religious rituals were performed.

The Incas of Peru also built superbly in stone. Inca masonry, in which no mortar was used, is of astonishing precision. This achievement is even more astounding since the Incas had no metal tools. A few examples remain today. At Cuzco, once the capital of the Inca Empire, is the fortress of Sacsahuamán. It was built in the fifteenth century as a symbol of the strength of the Incas as much as a fortification. The ruins of Machu Picchu, high in the Andes Mountains, were discovered earlier this century. Machu Picchu was an Inca town that was virtually inaccessible and so was probably used as a retreat. The buildings are cleverly incorporated with outcrops of rock, so the town seems to grow out of the mountain.

But these early American civilizations, including their architecture, were to be eclipsed by the civilization of Europe—which, by the time Machu Picchu was built, around the end of the fifteenth century, had reached a high stage of development.

Above *Simplicity is an important feature of the interior of Japanese houses. The low furniture is carefully arranged, and the sliding paper screens open to reveal other rooms.*

Below *The Castillo of Kukulcan, at Chichén Itzá, Mexico.*

4 Castles and Cathedrals

When we think of the Middle Ages in Europe in architectural terms, two images come to mind: the castle, with its massive walls, turrets, and battlements, and the Gothic cathedral, with its soaring vaults and stained glass windows. Other important kinds of buildings were constructed during this period, but these two reflect, in their grandeur and complexity, the sophisticated and powerful societies that were established in Europe around the beginning of the eleventh century.

During the preceding 500 years, relatively little architecture had been produced in Christian Europe. The Emperor Charlemagne, who reigned from 768–814, had built some churches and palaces, basing them on Roman and Byzantine models; but this brief renaissance, together with Charlemagne's empire itself, was subsequently extinguished by barbarian invasions.

As a measure of political stability was gradually reestablished, kings and powerful lords built castles, from which they could defend their territories. The early castles were motte and bailey castles. They

Left *The pilgrimage Church of Ste. Madeleine, at Vézelay, France, built in the early twelfth century, is a blend of Romanesque and Gothic architecture. The nave has the characteristically Romanesque round arches and barrel vault, but the choir is built in the simple, yet graceful, early Gothic style.*

Left *Like many other castles along the Rhine, Burg Stahleck, at Bacharach, has been restored in recent times. However, its lofty position and grim appearance reflect the serious function such castles served when stretches of the Rhine were fiercely disputed by neighboring lords.*

Below *The keep of Rochester Castle, Kent, which was completed in 1139, is a fine example of an early medieval castle. Among its defensive features are the crenellation at the top and the round tower guarding the entrance.*

consisted of a wooden tower set within a court, or bailey, on top of an earthen mound, or motte. From these the tall, fortified keep developed; this contained living quarters for the lord, his family, and his retainers. This was surrounded by a wall and a moat, which provided the first and second lines of defense. Round towers projecting from the wall at intervals enabled those defending the castle to fire from the side at the enemy. The crenellation on the top of the wall gave some protection to those facing the attackers head-on.

Although the design of castles was governed by practical considerations, the results were often visually exciting, even beautiful. Among the most splendid and best-fortified castles were those built in Wales by King Edward I of England (who reigned 1272–1307) to keep his newly conquered subjects in line. The last of these, Beaumaris, has two encircling walls and a symmetrical plan.

Castles with a more romantic aspect include those built along the banks of the Rhine River, in Germany. Asymmetrically designed, they seem to grow out of the rocks on which they were built.

Many of the churches built in the early Middle Ages resemble fortresses in some respects, with their massive walls pierced by slitlike windows and their heavy cylindrical columns. This style, which is known as Romanesque, evolved, as the name suggests, from Roman models and includes features such as round arches, vaults, and domes.

Early Christian architecture had rejected the form of the Roman temple, with its columned porticoes, because of its pagan associations. Instead, churches were modeled on the Roman basilica, which, being a nonreligious building, was neutral. These churches consisted of a simple rectangular hall, usually with side aisles formed by colonnades. Behind the altar there might be a semicircular, domed apse, in which the clergy sat while not officiating.

The Romanesque church evolved from this early basilica form. The two most obvious developments were the lengthening of the apse and the replacement of the basilica's flat wooden roof with a barrel vault. By enlarging the apse and further differentiating it from the rest of the church, it was possible to accommodate a choir. Music was becoming an increasingly important part of Christian worship at that time. In addition, many of the most important churches in Europe were attached to monasteries and abbeys, and so it was necessary to provide separate areas within the church for the monks and the members of the lay congregation.

The stone barrel, or tunnel, vault—which is really just an extended round arch—not only offered protection against fire but also provided wonderful acoustics for the traditional Gregorian chant. A further development was the cross vault, in which two semicircular arches cross at right angles. This is a lighter structure than the barrel vault, which means that the supporting walls of the church can be slightly thinner. Vaults began also to be constructed with ribs, which formed the main support, allowing the areas between to be filled with a lighter-weight stone.

The generally heavy aspect of Romanesque architecture was lightened by decorating the churches, inside and out, with sculpture. The capitals of the smooth columns were often deeply incised with gracefully swirling patterns of vines and leaves and fanciful representations of animals, or scenes from the Bible. The door frames were often carved with abstract patterns—zigzags, for example, were especially popular in England.

All this time, forms of church worship were becoming increasingly elaborate. Various saints became the object of special devotions, and so chapels were built and dedicated to them. Some churches also possessed relics of saints, which attracted pilgrims from distant places. To accommodate these worshipers, ambulatories were built. An ambulatory is an aisle that runs behind the choir and leads to the chapels where the relics were kept. Still more chapels and worshipers necessitated the addition of sideway extensions, called transepts. So the plan of the church took on the form of a Latin cross—which not only served a practical function but also had an obvious symbolic value for Christians.

The growing complexity of this plan, however, raised problems in its construction. In order to vault areas of different shapes and of different heights, the semicircular arch had to be abandoned in favor of the pointed arch. The angle of the pointed arch could be adjusted to span the required distance. At the same time, builders began to realize the possibility of dispensing with thick walls, since the columns could carry most of the weight.

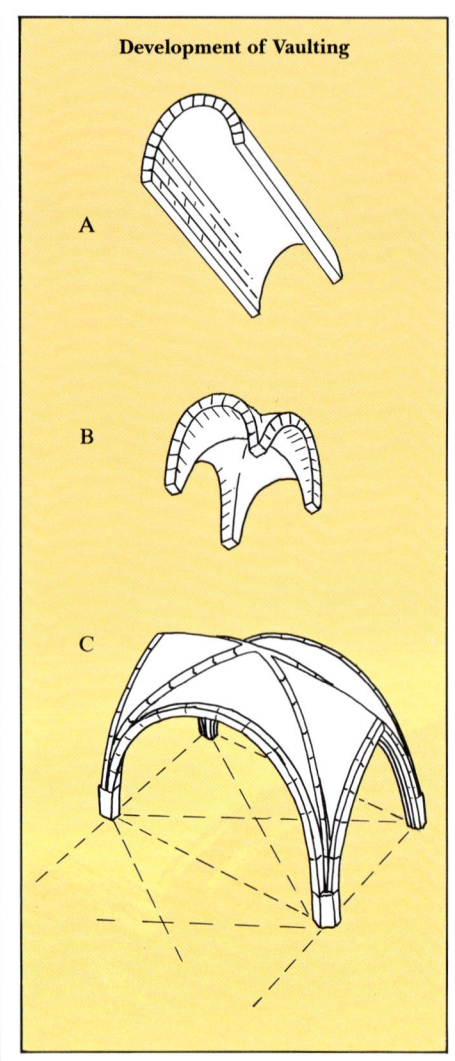

Development of Vaulting

Above *These drawings show how the construction of vaults became more complicated during the Middle Ages. The* **barrel vault** *(A) (also called a tunnel vault) is simply a round arch extended. A* **groin vault** *(B) is the intersection, at right angles, of two barrel vaults. The* **Gothic rib vault** *(C) is based on the pointed arch, which can be made wider or narrower with no change in height. This allows arches of different widths to intersect.*

Inset right *The Cathedral of Notre Dame, Paris, is one of the most harmonious of all Gothic cathedrals. The flying buttresses that support the apse are particularly graceful. Typical of French Gothic is the delicate spire (called a flèche, or "arrow") over the crossing.*

The vault, however, still exerted an outward as well as downward thrust. This was countered by one of the most brilliant inventions in the history of architecture: the flying buttress. This consists of an exterior arch that joins the upper part of the wall at the clerestory to a vertical buttress and conducts the thrust of the vault safely to the ground. Flying buttresses manage to heighten the impression of weightlessness conveyed by a building.

Below *The splendid Ca d'Oro derives its name (Golden House) from the fact that when it was built, in the fifteenth century, parts of its colored marble façade were decorated with gold leaf. The sensuous quality of the stone tracery is typical of Venetian Gothic.*

Above *The magnificent stone tracery and stained glass window in the west façade of Reims Cathedral, in northern France. The cathedral was begun in the mid-thirteenth century by Bernard de Soissons and completed in the fifteenth century.*

Even to modern eyes, the great Gothic cathedrals are awe-inspiring. For a medieval peasant, whose normal surroundings were a mud and thatch hut with the simplest furnishings, to enter such a place must have been an overwhelming experience. The soaring vaults, the lacy foliage carved in stone, and above all, the glorious jewel-like windows, must have seemed like a foretaste of Paradise.

This was, of course, the intended effect. "Man may rise to the contemplation of the divine through the senses," wrote Abbot Suger, under whose direction the Abbey Church of St. Denis, near Paris, was transformed in the mid-1100s to become the first example of the new style. The Abbot deliberately set out to make his church an earthly representation of divine light.

From France the new style—not called Gothic until centuries later— spread quickly to other parts of Europe. As it traveled, it was modified in various ways. In France, for example, emphasis was given to height, but in England length and complex patterns of vaulting were important. In Central Europe, also, the ribs of vaults were arranged very decoratively, often forming star and floral patterns.

Toward the end of the fourteenth century there was a tendency toward delicacy in the arts generally. In France this was evident in the late phase of Gothic called *Flamboyant*. It was named after the flamelike curves of the stone window tracery. In England, a new, lighter effect was achieved using larger windows, gently curved at the top and scored with strong vertical tracery. The verticality of the style, known as Perpendicular, was emphasized even more by the great square towers placed over the crossing of many churches, although this effect was softened by the beautiful fan vaulting. These generously curved, conical shapes, with their rich yet delicate tracery, are unique to England.

The enormous expense and labor involved in building a great Gothic church meant that in most cases work was carried out over many years. As a result, many of these churches incorporate styles from different periods. Although this detracts from the unity of the effect, it does enhance the sense of organic development and the interest for the student of architecture. Fascinating contrasts can be found even in so harmonious a building as Chartres Cathedral, in northern France, most of which was built within about sixty years. Here, the sober lines of the early south bell tower, built about 1170, complement the *Flamboyant* flourishes of the spire on the north tower, added in the early sixteenth century.

Although originally conceived as a religious architecture, the Gothic style was adapted for use in all of the important kinds of medieval building. Castles, town halls, university buildings, all had rib-vaulted halls, windows with pointed arches, and roofs punctuated with intricately carved pinnacles. The townhouses of nobility and rich merchants also included Gothic features—especially in Venice, where the style took on a highly sensuous quality, particularly in the lacy arcades adorning some of the palaces along the Grand Canal.

5 A Sense of Proportion

In central and southern Italy the Gothic style never developed to the extent that it did north of the Alps, or even in Spain. However, in the northern cities, such as Milan, there was a program of cathedral building in the eleventh century that was in the Gothic style and patronized by the ruling families. In central and southern Italy the Romanesque traditions of the rounded arch and the plain, cylindrical column remained dominant.

By the early fifteenth century, more ancient artistic traditions—those of the Classical world—were being rediscovered in central Italy. This movement, which we call the Renaissance, began in the city of Florence, and so it is not surprising that the authorities supervising the building of that city's mainly Gothic cathedral decided to crown it with a form derived from antiquity: a dome. This dome, however, was unlike any ever seen before. It rested on an octagonal base, and was ingeniously constructed with an inner and an outer shell, and a complex system of ribs and arches.

Above *The Cathedral of Florence was given its distinctive dome by Filippo Brunelleschi in the fifteenth century. Most of the cathedral is built in the colorful fusion of Gothic and Romanesque, typical of central Italy.*

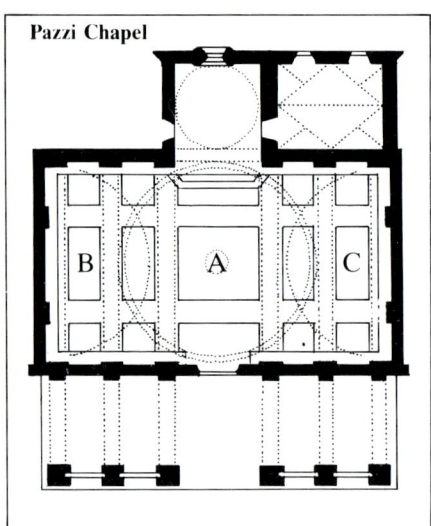

Above *The symmetry characteristic of Italian Renaissance architecture can be seen in this plan of Brunelleschi's Pazzi Chapel. The rectangular main area subdivides into a central square (A), covered with a dome, and two barrel-vaulted ends (B) and (C).*

Opposite *Classical features—columns, pilasters, and a frieze—were included in the graceful design for this arcade in the courtyard of the Ducal Palace at Urbino, in northern Italy.*

Below *Bramante's Tempietto, Rome.*

The designer of this extraordinary structure was Filippo Brunelleschi (1377–1446). He was one of a new breed of architects who, in the spirit of the Renaissance, studied Classical architecture and applied its principles to their own work. Brunelleschi's mastery of Classical principles can be seen very clearly in the beautiful chapel (1429–46) built for the Pazzi family in the cloister of Santa Croce in Florence. It is centrally planned, and the harmony of the chapel's interior is achieved through a subtle, yet simple, relationship of squares, rectangles, domes, and barrel vaults. These are articulated by gray stone pilasters and moldings against white plastered walls. The proportions of the chapel are all mathematically exact; for instance, the square under the central dome measures half the total width of the building (see diagram left).

Renaissance ideals of proportion were formed from what was known of Classical models. The books of the Roman architect Vitruvius (active 46–30 B.C.) were the only surviving text on the architecture of ancient Rome. They were consulted with renewed enthusiasm, and were translated into modern European languages and illustrated with measured drawings of Roman buildings. Vitruvius was to be a major source of inspiration and an authority for architects in the centuries that followed. The Renaissance architect Leon Battista Alberti (1404–72), for example, based his treatise, *De re aedificatoria (On the Art of Building)*, on the work of Vitruvius. Beauty in architecture, Alberti stated, was "the harmony and concord of all the parts achieved in such a manner that nothing could be added, or taken away, or altered except for the worse." Like his contemporaries, Alberti believed that this harmony could be achieved by combining basic geometric forms such as the square and cube (which might be halved or doubled) and the circle and sphere, and by keeping to simple proportions such as 1:1, 1:2, and 2:3.

Along with Classical proportions, the structural and decorative features of ancient Greek and Roman architecture were reintroduced. For example, Alberti gave his Church of Sant' Andrea, in Mantua, Italy, a splendid coffered barrel vault, and the windows were surmounted by triangular and curved pediments.

Any remaining prejudice against using such forms for churches was far outweighed by the conviction that Classical forms reflected the divine order in the Universe. On the spot in Rome where St. Peter was believed to have been martyred, the architect Donato Bramante (1444–1514) built the Tempietto, a tiny circular chapel surrounded by a Tuscan colonnade and crowned by a dome. A model of proportion, the Tempietto is generally regarded as the Renaissance building that most faithfully imitated the Classical world.

Bramante was as fascinated by the central plan as were most Renaissance architects, and when he was commissioned to design a new church to replace the old St. Peter's basilica, in Rome, he planned it in the form of a Greek cross within a square. After his death, a number of different architects worked on St. Peter's, and eventually Bramante's

original plan was modified to the traditional Latin cross, which was better suited to Christian worship.

Among the architects who contributed to the design of St. Peter's was Michelangelo Buonarroti (1475–1564). This genius was not the man to follow rules in a slavish manner. Instead he took the Classical style and adapted it to suit his own purposes and vision. The highly sculptural quality of his architecture can be seen in the east end of St. Peter's. The exterior has a molded, or "plastic," character, made even more striking by the use of huge pilasters rising up through two stories. Introduced by Michelangelo, the "giant order," as it is called, was soon adopted by other Renaissance architects. Michelangelo himself used the giant order, combined with columns of different sizes, on the façades of three palaces he designed to flank a square on the Capitoline Hill, in Rome. This elegant piazza epitomizes Renaissance ideas of balance and harmony in city planning.

Perhaps even more influential than Michelangelo, in the long term, was the work of Andrea Palladio (1508–80). Palladio worked mainly in the Veneto, the part of Italy around Venice. Here, he built several grand townhouses, two superb churches, and many villas. In these coolly elegant country houses Palladio developed his own interpretation of Classicism, which was marked by symmetry, harmonious proportions (based on musical intervals), and a strong sense of hierarchy. This can be seen in the relative importance given to each part of the buildings. Most of the villas, for example, consist of a central block with a portico to give it additional importance, flanked by low wings that contain the kitchen, servants' quarters, and other subordinate elements. The idea of giving a house a temple front was a new one, but it has proved to be one of the most popular themes in the history of architecture, for it appears on both sides of the Atlantic.

Below *Built in the early 1500s, the Château of Chenonceau illustrates the fusion of Renaissance and medieval styles in sixteenth-century French architecture. The basically symmetrical forms of its two parts and the cool serenity of the Grande Galerie, poised over the Cher River, coexist harmoniously with the romantically medieval spires and turrets.*

Above *One of Palladio's masterpieces, the Church of San Giorgio Maggiore, in Venice, shows his masterful adaptation of Classical forms. The façade consists basically of two interlocking temple fronts, each with its own pediment. The lower of these spans the side aisles of the interior, while the higher ascends to the greater height of the nave. Correct Classical proportions are maintained by raising the central attached columns onto pedestals—a device repeated inside the church.*

Many of Palladio's villas were built for working farms and have extensive outbuildings; but the most famous of them, the Villa Rotonda, outside Vicenza, was designed as a retreat. Palladian influence can be seen in the interior of King's Chapel, Boston, and in many mansions in the southern United States.

Palladio's two great Venetian churches, San Giorgio Maggiore and Il Redentore, show how he was able to adapt the form of a Classical temple front and apply it successfully to the façade of a Christian church, maintaining Classical proportions at the same time. The higher pediment, at the level of the nave, rests on columns raised on pedestals. The lower pediment, at the height of the aisles, is supported by columns standing on the ground.

North of the Alps, the principles and forms of Classicism were applied only cautiously at first and piecemeal. In the exquisite French châteaux and stately English Tudor manor houses of the sixteenth century, regular plans and occasional Classical motifs were combined with native traditions such as steep roofs, dormers, and bay windows. Renaissance ideas of town-planning were expressed in the elegant Place Royal (now the Place des Vosges), in Paris, completed in 1612. This harmoniously designed square is said to have inspired the first great English Classical architect, Inigo Jones (1573–1652), in the design of London's Covent Garden. Although the original Covent Garden has now been altered beyond recognition, the simple Tuscan portico of Jones' St. Paul's Church gives this lively square an element of serene, classical dignity.

6 Splendor and Elegance

Once rediscovered by Renaissance architects in the early 1400s, Classical forms were to dominate Western architecture, on and off, for the following 400 years. During that time architects demonstrated how the Classical style could be adapted to suit a great variety of buildings. Today, after decades of glass and concrete boxes, Classical forms are making a tentative comeback.

By the middle of the sixteenth century, as we have already seen, architects such as Michelangelo and Palladio were handling these forms more freely, in order to discover their expressive possibilities. The following century was to see this process accelerated to produce the extravagant style called Baroque.

Baroque architecture first appeared in Rome, in the work of Gianlorenzo Bernini (1598–1680) and his rival Francesco Borromini (1599–1667). In the buildings designed by both these men, the keynote is high drama. They made use of all the Classical forms, columns, pilasters, and pediments, but they did not obey the Classical rules. Some of their churches, for instance, are built on oval ground plans, with façades that bulge and curve. Inside, the domed or coved ceilings are decorated with rich coffering or with paintings of airborne saints and cherubs. Walls erupt with sculpture, from ornamental floral festoons, or swags, and angels blowing trumpets, to dramatic depictions of the mystical experiences of the saints.

The Baroque style was an expression of the new religious fervor within the Roman Catholic Church. After the upheaval of the Protestant Reformation in the sixteenth century, the Church reasserted its teachings with a direct appeal to the emotions. The overwhelming splendor of Baroque art and architecture was the visual complement to this religious revival. It found a natural home in other Catholic countries besides Italy. In Spain, and in Spanish America, the style became extremely elaborate, dense, and heavy. In Austria and southern Germany it often took on a giddy exuberance, in which the profusion of gilding and colored marble was lightened by large, clear windows and white walls.

France, although predominantly Catholic, did not embrace the Baroque style quite so fervently as its neighbors. French Baroque architecture was tempered by a measure of Classical formality. But in this relatively restrained form, the Baroque style was admirably suited to proclaiming the majesty of kings, as can be seen in the magnificent palace at Versailles, built for Louis XIV, the "Sun King."

Lesser princes, too, were quick to exploit the symbolic value of the Baroque. For example, the Prince-Bishop of Würzburg, in Germany,

Right *The highly ornate façade of Santiago de Compostela, in Spain, was added to this medieval cathedral in the early eighteenth century. The profusion of curved lines and the lavishly applied ornament showed Spanish Baroque at its most florid.*

Above *The delicate decorative plasterwork, with painted and gilded details and cherubs, on the ceiling of the Church of Vierzehnheiligen, in southern Germany, is typical of the Rococo style.*

Below *The north front of Castle Howard, Yorkshire, by the architect (and playwright) Sir John Vanbrugh, illustrates the relatively sedate form of Baroque found in England.*

commissioned the Court architect, Balthasar Neumann (1687–1753) to build his Residenz in a suitably grandiose manner. Inside, Neumann designed a majestic staircase that leads to magnificent public rooms on the first floor. Above the staircase is an astonishing painted ceiling depicting four of the continents by the Italian painter Giambattista Teipolo (1696–1770) whose fame grew outside his native Italy. The Baroque decoration is well suited to a setting intended for spectacle and ceremony.

Some of Neumann's best work is in the Rococo style. This is a lighter, frothier version of the Baroque, using asymmetrical, swirling curves, often based on shell and floral motifs. It was originally a French development, applied mainly to interiors. The interior of Neumann's church of Vierzehnheiligen (Fourteen Saints), started in 1743, is a delightfully joyous example of the Rococo style. There are echoes of the Classical origins of Baroque architecture in the columns and pilasters. In the Rococo salons of palaces and townhouses, however, the Classical orders disappeared, and were replaced with beautifully carved, curved panels.

In England, the Baroque style retained a strong Classical element. The churches built by Sir Christopher Wren (1632–1723) have some Baroque features, such as curved porches and arched windows crowned with ornamental garlands. Many of these churches have elaborate steeples, made up of tiers of columns and arches—a Baroque treatment of a medieval form. But these Anglican churches are restrained when compared with the full-blown Catholic Baroque style found on the continent.

Left *The Petit Trianon (begun 1762) at Versailles shows French Neoclassicism at its most refined. The beautifully proportioned casement windows are typically French.*

Below *The tiered Baroque steeple of St. Bride's Church, designed by Sir Christopher Wren, is one of London's landmarks. Wren designed more than fifty London churches, including his masterpiece, St. Paul's Cathedral.*

The great houses designed by Sir John Vanbrugh (1664–1726) are based more firmly in the Baroque tradition. Blenheim Palace (begun in 1705) and Castle Howard (built 1699–1712) are two huge palaces that he designed to incorporate a complex mixture of curving and rectangular shapes and elaborately detailed façades. They impose a self-conscious grandeur on the gently rolling English landscape.

As the eighteenth century progressed, there was a move away from Baroque excess toward a more restrained Classicism, more in keeping with the spirit of the Age of Reason. Architects and young noblemen from northern Europe flocked to Italy to see for themselves the marvels of antiquity and the Renaissance, and later applied these discoveries in new building at home.

When the British aristocracy discovered Palladio's villas, many a noble lord had his own dignified Palladian-style country house, with a raised portico, rusticated ground floor, and flanking pavilions. Then, toward the end of the century, the more richly decorative style of Neoclassicism developed by Robert Adam (1728–92) became fashionable. Adam is particularly known for his beautiful interiors, which feature exquisite moldings and subtle color schemes.

In continental Europe, also, the Neoclassical trend produced some elegant buildings—none more elegant than the Petit Trianon. This small retreat, built for Louis XV at Versailles, was designed by the *Premier Architecte* Ange-Jacques Gabriel (1698–1782).

At the same time, towns and cities in Europe were given a new orderliness and dignity, at least in the more prosperous neighborhoods, as regular patterns of streets and squares replaced the haphazard development of earlier centuries. The spatial contrast experienced when walking through an eighteenth-century neighborhood, from street to square to crescent, is one of the elements that make these towns so pleasing. The harmony of the architecture itself is important, too. The noble proportions of the row houses that line the streets and squares of Edinburgh's New Town in Scotland, for

Above *The Royal Crescent, Bath. Designed by John Wood the Younger and completed in 1775, this elliptical terrace of thirty townhouses, built in mellow Bath stone, forms part of a rhythmic sequence of streets and open spaces in this elegant Georgian city.*

example, or those of Bath, in the west of England, are proof that repetition can be visually satisfying.

The coolly restrained, simple style of British Neoclassicism, commonly called Georgian, after the Hanoverian kings who reigned during this period, followed the flag to the American colonies. There it later became known as Colonial. Fine examples of Georgian townhouses can be seen in such eastern cities as Boston, Philadelphia, and the restored eighteenth-century town of Williamsburg, Virginia. The landed gentry of the southern colonies were just as devoted to classical principles as their European cousins, and they built their plantation houses with careful attention to proportion and symmetry. The portico here acquired a practical function, serving as a pleasant place to sit in the hot summer months.

When the time came to choose a suitable style of architecture for the new American republic, the Founding Fathers turned to Classical models again. They were guided by Thomas Jefferson (1743–1826), who was himself an amateur architect of some distinction. Jefferson's design for the new Virginia State Capitol, in Richmond, was derived from the Maison Carrée (16 B.C.), at Nîmes, which he had admired while visiting southern France.

Significantly, Jefferson's building has Ionic columns instead of the Corinthian ones used on the Maison Carrée. By this time, Neoclassicism had entered the phase known as Greek Revival. The simpler orders of Greece's Golden Age, especially the severe, comparatively squat Greek Doric, had become more popular. Greek Classicism struck just the right democratic, idealistic note for the new nation, and it soon became established as the most appropriate for American public buildings, and for many private houses as well.

In Europe, too, the Greek Revival style was in keeping with the liberal, progressive ideals of the time. Thus, it was found especially suitable for schools and for museums. Berlin's Altes Museum, designed by Karl Friedrich Schinkel (1781–1841), with its monumental, absolutely straight Greek colonnade, perfectly expresses the intellectual purpose of the institution it houses.

7 Something Old, Something New

The purity of style characteristic of the Greek Revival of the early 1800s was to be short-lived. In the late eighteenth century the picturesque and the exotic were becoming popular alternatives. In England and Germany, a few Gothic-style houses had been built; and the English architect John Nash (1752–1835), known mainly for his Neoclassical buildings, had transformed the Prince Regent's residence in Brighton into a would-be Indian fantasy. As the century progressed, architects and their patrons in both Europe and the United States seemed to be indulging in a sort of architectural costume ball, as one style after another—Neo-Gothic, Neo-Italian Renaissance, Neo-Byzantine, and Neo-Baroque—was tried on.

Of all these styles, Gothic was to enjoy the greatest popularity in the United States and Great Britain. It had many favorable associations. For the romantics of the early 1800s, it conjured up an idealized vision of the Middle Ages, with its code of chivalry and knightly valor. For the devout it represented the medieval Age of Faith. For the founders of new American universities it was a link with the academic traditions of Oxford and Cambridge. With its overtones of a glorious past and, at the same time, spiritual strivings, it perfectly suited the confident, idealistic Victorian mentality.

Above *Brighton Pavilion (1815–21), the work of John Nash, is the outstanding example of that architect's flair for picturesque effects. Nash worked in many styles, and the novel exotic qualities characteristic of his buildings were to reappear in the work of many other architects throughout the nineteenth century.*

Above *St. Patrick's Cathedral, New York, stands in full Neo-Gothic splendor, surrounded by skyscrapers.*

Below *St. Pancras Hotel, London, was designed by Sir George Gilbert Scott (1811–78) in full-blown Victorian Gothic. The rich red-brick exterior, with its soaring spires and pinnacles, is complemented by the luxurious interior.*

When the British Houses of Parliament burned down in 1834, it was decided that they should be rebuilt in the Gothic style. The regular plan of the Palace of Westminster actually owes a great deal to the Classical traditions favored by its main architect, Sir Charles Barry (1795–1860). Its Gothic appearance is the work of Barry's collaborator, Augustus Welby Northmore Pugin (1812–52), a fervent, even fanatical, admirer of the Gothic style. He clothed Barry's basic structure in a profusion of medieval moldings, traceries, and spires.

Churches, of course, were the ideal candidates for the Gothic style and splendid examples were created in the United States and Great Britain until well into this century. St. Patrick's Cathedral, in New York, completed in 1889, is reminiscent of French Gothic churches. English Victorian-Gothic churches reveled in color and pattern, with multicolored tiled floors and blue-painted starry vaults.

As in the Middle Ages, the Gothic style was freely adapted to all sorts of other buildings, including private houses. The increasingly prosperous middle-class world loved its potential flamboyance, and many an affluent businessman had built for himself a so-called medieval pile of towers and battlements, with vast rooms and stained glass windows around the front door.

One of the most spectacular examples of Victorian Gothic is the St. Pancras Hotel, in London. Nowadays the building is used as offices, but this colorful red-brick extravaganza, with its steep roof, punctuated by rows of spiky dormers, and its lavishly decorated interior, once provided visitors to London with a taste of living like a medieval baron, but with "modern" Victorian comforts.

Apart from a few striking examples, such as Ludwig II's castle of Neuchwanstein, in Bavaria (completed 1886), the Gothic Revival never had quite the same popularity in continental Europe as it did in the United States and Great Britain. Instead, the taste for the grandiose was satisfied by other styles. In France, for example, there emerged the style known as Second Empire, named for the Emperor Napoleon III (who reigned 1852–70). A highly florid style, based on the Baroque, this can be seen today in town halls throughout France. Many American architects studied in Paris, at the École des Beaux Arts, and so the Second Empire style spread to the United States. The Executive Office Building, in Washington, D.C., is a perfect example of this style.

Ever since the first operas were composed, early in the seventeenth century, the design of opera houses has provided architects with opportunities to exercise their skill at creating dramatic effects. As the most spectacular form of theater, opera demanded an appropriately spectacular setting—as did the elegant people who attended it. Jean-Louis Charles Garnier (1825–98) applied this principle with dazzling success. His Paris Opéra (completed in 1874) is the most famous example of the Second Empire style. It is the most sumptuous opera house ever built, and it is also extremely well planned, with spacious foyers and grand staircases designed to enhance the sense of occasion for those attending performances.

Equally successful, although in a totally different way, is another public building in Paris, the Bibliothèque Ste. Geneviève. This was designed by Henri Labrouste (1801–75) and completed in 1850. Its simple façade, Classical in spirit, is articulated by two stories of arched windows and engraved with the names of 810 renowned authors—a visible sign of the library's function. The spacious reading room has a double barrel-vaulted ceiling, supported by slender columns made of cast iron.

The introduction of cast iron as a building material opened up new possibilities in building design. Factories had been built with iron frames as early as the 1790s. Later, great sheds of iron and glass were constructed for the new railroad stations. Many of these remarkable feats of engineering can still be admired today. The Crystal Palace, however, has not survived. It was built in London's Hyde Park to house the Great Exhibition of 1851. This enormous prefabricated structure, designed by Joseph Paxton (1801–65), made of iron and glass, measuring 1,847 feet long, was destroyed in a fire in 1936.

More famous than the Crystal Palace is the Eiffel Tower. This great iron structure, built for the Paris Exhibition of 1889, has now become the symbol of Paris. By the time the Eiffel Tower was built, the cast-iron frame, and then the steel frame, were being used in the building of office buildings. Together with the invention of the elevator—first used in an office building in New York in 1871—this new technology made it possible to add floor after floor to a building, without making it too heavy to stand. This would have been impossible with a stone or brick construction. And so the skyscraper was born.

Below *The interior of the Crystal Palace (1851). This magnificent achievement in design and technology was designed, tested, and built in nine months.*

The first skyscrapers were built in Chicago. The fire of 1870 had destroyed much of that city, and the abundance of work to be done there attracted a number of forward-looking architects. The most famous of this Chicago school of architects was Louis Henry Sullivan (1856–1924). Besides being one of the pioneers of steel frame construction, Sullivan was the first architect to develop an appropriate aesthetic for the office building. The façades of his buildings are designed so that they express the frame behind them.

The use of metal construction took on a completely different character in the style called Art Nouveau, which emerged in the 1890s. Like its counterparts in the decorative arts, this style of architecture featured wavy plantlike motifs and subtle colors. The style was popular in Europe generally, but perhaps the best examples can be seen in Brussels, in Belgium.

The most extravagant interpretations of Art Nouveau can be seen in Barcelona, Spain, in the buildings designed by Antoni Gaudí (1852–1926). The surging, organic forms of Gaudí's buildings, which include some apartment buildings and the unfinished Church of the Sagrada Familia (Holy Family) contradict all accepted notions about building since humans first emerged from their caves.

Gaudí's contemporary, the Scottish artist and architect Charles Rennie Mackintosh (1868–1928), represents the other extreme of Art Nouveau. His designs are spare, vertical, and basically rectangular, though still imbued with delicacy and a great sensitivity to the sensuous qualities of materials, different types of wood in particular. Mackintosh had a greater reputation abroad, especially in Vienna where his work was very influential, than at home; but today the originality of his designs is universally recognized.

Right *There is scarcely a right angle to be found in Casa Milá, an apartment building in Barcelona designed by Antoni Gaudí. Although it lacks the linear quality of true Art Nouveau, Casa Milá embodies the organic aspect of this style; it seems not to have been constructed but to have grown out of the earth.*

8 Modern Lines

The dominant architectural image of the twentieth century is the glass and concrete box. Rectangular and without any ornament, it is so familiar a sight that we have forgotten how revolutionary it once was. Only in the past few years has its claim to be *the* modern architecture been effectively challenged.

Today, this style of architecture—called either Functionalism, Modernism, or the International Style—is being widely attacked for its insensitivity and, in many respects, its surprising impracticality. For instance, flat roofs are prone to leaking, and concrete tends to discolor. It is worthwhile remembering, however, that a good many other styles besides Modernism have flourished in this century.

The Modernist style first emerged in continental Europe just before World War I (1914–18). At the time, it seemed like the embodiment of a wonderful new vision of the future, free of the trappings of past ages, cleansed of class distinctions, and based on purity of line and a straightforward expression of structure. In the Netherlands, a group of architects associated with a movement called De Stijl drew their inspiration from the rectangular, linear paintings of Piet Mondrian (1872–1944).

In Germany, a similarly purist approach was being developed at the Bauhaus, a school of arts and crafts at Dessau. Under the direction of Walter Gropius (1883–1969) and, later, Ludwig Mies van der Rohe (1886–1969), the Bauhaus became the center of Modernism. The building itself, designed by Gropius and completed in 1926, exemplifies the Functionalist principles of the movement. Gropius carefully avoided giving his building any of the symbolic overtones associated with schools. There are no visual references to Classical

Below *When it was completed in 1930, Le Corbusier's Villa Savoye was startlingly avant-garde. Built of reinforced concrete, severely plain, it was conceived by its architect as "a machine for living in." The small ground floor, behind the* pilotis *(columns), includes an entrance hall, servant's room, and garage; the main rooms and a terrace occupy the second floor.*

traditions or the medieval cloister; instead, the classrooms, workshops, and auditorium are contained within several asymmetrically grouped blocks, built of smooth, undecorated, reinforced concrete with large areas of glass.

The work of the other great Bauhaus architect, Mies van der Rohe, is noted for its extreme simplicity. "Less is more," said Mies; and in his best work he made a convincing case for this observation. Later in his career, in the United States, Mies produced the kind of sleekly elegant skyscraper that other architects imitated but rarely equaled. The most famous is New York's Seagram Building (1958), which Mies designed in collaboration with Philip Johnson (b. 1906).

The bronze and the brown-tinted glass used for the Seagram Building reflects Mies's liking of rich materials, which was already evident in his German Pavilion for the Barcelona Exhibition of 1929. The pavilion, since demolished, was a masterly arrangement of planes, in glass, green marble, and a creamy stone called travertine, conveying a mood of great serenity.

At about the same time, the Swiss-born architect Le Corbusier (1887–1965) was developing his concept of a house as "a machine for living in," free of any superficial or symbolic elements. His ideas were expressed most lucidly in a series of houses he built in northern France. Constructed of reinforced concrete, these houses are essentially cubes, from which some parts have been cut away. In some cases, the main story is supported partly on slender columns, called *pilotis*. The windows are horizontal, ribbonlike slits, and the roofs are flat, some serving as terraces.

Later, Le Corbusier was to apply his Functionalist principles on a larger scale, to such buildings as the Unité d'Habitation (1952), in Marseilles. This massive 18-story building contains more than 300 apartments, as well as shops, and other communal facilities. Built of rough-finished concrete and supported by squat, spreading *pilotis*, the Unité d'Habitation served as a model for many postwar public housing projects.

While Modernism went from strength to strength in Europe, it made little impact on Britain until after World War II. The leading British architect of the prewar years, Sir Edwin Lutyens (1869–1944), drew on Classical and traditional English architectural themes in his dignified office buildings and gracious country houses. Lutyens' masterpiece, the Viceroy's House (1931), in New Delhi, India, brilliantly incorporates Classical and Indian motifs.

In the United States, the design of skyscrapers provided a new challenge for architects. Skyscrapers of the 1920s and early 1930s were often embellished with Art Deco designs. A style mostly associated with furnishings, Art Deco consists of streamlined shapes, often with echoes of Egyptian or Moorish art. The outstanding example of the Art Deco skyscraper is New York's Chrysler Building, designed by William Van Alen (1883–1954), which is crowned by a series of scalloped shapes incised with a jagged sunburst pattern.

Above *The main façade of the Viceroy's House in New Delhi (1915–24) by Sir Edwin Lutyens. Designed to symbolize the authority of British rule in India, it combines Classical and Indian forms, as can be seen in the dome over the entrance.*

Above *Le Corbusier's Chapel of Notre-Dame-du-Haut, at Ronchamp, France, is as much a piece of sculpture as a building, and represents a dramatic departure from the boxlike character of Le Corbusier's earlier work.*

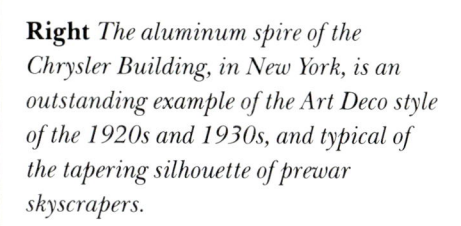

Right *The aluminum spire of the Chrysler Building, in New York, is an outstanding example of the Art Deco style of the 1920s and 1930s, and typical of the tapering silhouette of prewar skyscrapers.*

Such frivolity was to be short-lived. By the 1930s, Modernism was rapidly gaining supporters in the United States. The Bauhaus was closed by the Nazis in 1933, and Mies, Gropius, and others emigrated to America. This gave a tremendous boost to the Modernist movement in the United States.

There was, however, a conspicuous dissenter—Frank Lloyd Wright (1869–1959). Generally regarded as the most original of all American architects, Wright first made a reputation in the early 1900s in Chicago with his Prairie Houses. With their strong horizontality, gracefully interlocking forms and fluid plans, inspired partly by Japanese house design, these elegant houses perfectly express the American love of spaciousness.

While despising the Modernists' "boxes on stilts," Wright took their favorite material, reinforced concrete, and used it, along with stone, to create what many people consider one the most beautiful of all twentieth-century houses, Falling Water (1936). The house is set on a rocky woodland hillside in Pennsylvania, with its various levels cantilevered over a waterfall. It is now more than fifty years old but has lost none of its visual impact.

Even in the postwar years, when the glass and concrete slab reigned supreme, it was often challenged by more imaginative forms. The Finnish-American architect Eero Saarinen (1910–1961) succeeded in suggesting flight in the swooping lines of his Trans-World Airlines (TWA) Terminal, completed in 1962, at Kennedy Airport, and at the Dulles International Airport, outside Washington, D.C. (completed in 1963).

In his "Habitat" at Expo '67, in Montreal, Moshe Safdie (b. 1938) broke up the uniformity of the apartment building design by piling the apartments one on top of another in a seemingly random fashion, the result resembling a three-dimensional Cubist painting. Le Corbusier revealed a surprising capacity for highly expressive work—most notably in the chapel of Notre-Dame-du-Haut (1954), in northern France. This astonishing building resembles a giant piece of abstract sculpture. Its thick, curving concrete walls, pierced with an irregular scattering of small stained glass windows, support a great rolling brown concrete roof, the shape of which was inspired by a crab's shell.

Undoubtedly the most spectacular use of precast concrete is the Sydney Opera House, completed in 1973, designed by the Danish architect Jørn Utzon (b. 1918). The billowing white sails of this gravity-defying structure are a triumph of modern technology.

Nothing could be further in spirit from the Sydney Opera House than the aggressively Functionalist Pompidou Center, completed in 1977, in Paris. Taking to extremes the Modernist principle that a building should reveal its structure, the Center's architects, Richard

Above *"Falling Water," by Frank Lloyd Wright, is a daring feat of cantilevered construction, made of reinforced concrete and stone, and perfectly integrated with the surrounding landscape.*

Right *James Stirling's addition to the Staatsgalerie in Stuttgart, Germany. His design combines Classical elements with more modern features, including the serpentine sloping glass walls and the wide pink and blue railings.*

Rogers (b. 1933) and Renzo Piano (b. 1937), placed the building's working parts, including plumbing and heating pipes, and an escalator, outside the glass and steel frame. Rogers' firm has used the same shock tactics on the Lloyds Bank Building, completed in 1984, in the City of London, England's Wall Street.

Although a few architects still remain faithful to the Modernist aesthetic, it has clearly had its day. Postmodernism is the trend of the times. The Postmodernists are united chiefly by their rejection of what they consider the sterility of Modernism and by their playful use of traditional forms and motifs. Like their nineteenth-century predecessors, they raid the past for ideas, but with a cheerful, even impudent, irreverence. Egyptian, Oriental, Classical, and other elements are borrowed, bent, and blown up in a manner that often suggests parody. For example, Philip Johnson's new American Telephone and Telegraph (AT&T) skyscraper in Manhattan, completed in 1979, is crowned with a huge broken pediment, which makes it look like a gigantic piece of eighteenth-century furniture.

Another controversial example of Postmodernism, the Portland (Oregon) Public Services Building (1982), designed by Michael Graves (b. 1934), has something of the streamlining typical of the Art Deco style, and more than a passing resemblance to a juke box.

A bold use of color is characteristic of much Postmodernist architecture. Buildings are painted in all sorts of colors, combined sometimes with a freedom that comes as a shock after decades of sober neutrals. This contrast of colors is a hallmark of the work of the British architect James Stirling (b. 1926). Stirling's best-known building to date, an addition to the Staatsgalerie in Stuttgart, Germany, completed in 1983, combines patterned masonry, using warm pink stone, with details in steel, painted bright blue, red, and green. Its shape is varied, too, incorporating drum shapes, ramps, and a sloping, undulating wall of glass and steel. While drawing on earlier architectural styles, the architect has transformed them almost beyond recognition.

The Postmodernists often assert that their aim is to create buildings that people will find amusing and fun. This was the reason given recently, for example, for building a large British home improvement superstore in Egyptian style, with some Corinthian columns thrown in. In the meantime, other architects are turning to the past—specifically to Classicism—with a more reverent spirit. They feel that Classical proportions and forms have an enduring value that makes them just as appropriate in our own time as in the fifth century B.C. or the fifteenth century A.D.

It is difficult to get a perspective on the architecture of the present day. Is Modernism truly dead? Does the bewildering variety of mock-antique styles represent a loss of confidence in our own civilization—or a healthy respect for tradition? Will our descendants ridicule our buildings as we used to ridicule those of the Victorians, and pull them down? Or will they found historical societies to renovate and preserve them?

Above *The Pompidou Center, in Paris, is Modernism at its most aggressive, with the functional elements of the building displayed—brightly colored—on the outside.*

Below *The gracefully swooping lines of Eero Saarinen's Dulles Airport, near Washington, D.C., are an eloquent expression of flight.*

⑨ Learning to Look at Architecture

Like any of the arts, architecture can be studied on many levels. You may wish to study the history of architecture formally, or you may simply want to be able to look at buildings with a more knowledgeable eye. You might even decide to study to become an architect.

Looking at buildings

We all have instinctive reactions to buildings. We may call a building beautiful, ugly, bizarre, nondescript, imposing, inviting, and so on. By asking some specific questions about a building as you are looking at it, you can discover exactly why you like or dislike it. What's more, you may also discover certain things about it that will cause you to modify your first impression.

When you are looking at the outside of a building, ask yourself some of the following questions:

- What structural parts are visible from the outside? For example, are there any flying buttresses, columns, or gables? Is there a steel or timber frame or a dome?
- How are the windows positioned? For example, are there the same number of windows on each floor? Are they placed symmetrically on either side of the door? Are any of them blocked in? What shape are they—square, rectangular, round-topped, pointed? Is the door a prominent feature? If so, how has this been achieved?
- What kinds of decoration, if any, have been used on the façade? Is the decoration Classical—with columns, pilasters, pediments, for example? Or is it Gothic or Oriental perhaps? Does it seem to be in harmony with the building as a whole, or does it appear to have been stuck on as an afterthought? Try to look at the same building at different times of the day and see what effect light has on the façade and its details.
- What materials have been used? Do they appear to be old or new? Have the materials been painted or stained, or left in their natural state? Are there any interesting contrasts of texture—between rough and smooth finishes, for example?
- Finally, how does the building relate to its setting? Does it dominate its surroundings, or does it seem to blend into them? Does the style of the building fit in with the other buildings around it, or does it contrast or even clash with them?

Here are some questions to ask when you go inside various buildings.
- What sort of spatial qualities does the interior have? For example, does it consist of one large space, or has it been divided, or

articulated in interesting ways? If there are rooms, do they vary in size considerably? Are all the rooms partitioned with doors, or do some of them flow into each other in an open plan? Do the various rooms feel spacious, cozy, claustrophobic?
- What kind of ceilings are there—arched, domed, vaulted, beamed, flat, coffered? Are the ceilings decorated in any other way?
- Is there a staircase? If so, is it a prominent feature? Where does it lead to?
- Is the plan symmetrical or asymmetrical? Are the walls flat, or do they include features such as paneling, niches, or chimney mantels?
- How is the interior affected by different kinds of light? How well suited is the building to its function? For example, if it is a theater, are the sightlines to the stage good from most parts of the auditorium? Are the foyers and refreshment areas comfortable? If it is an office, is there adequate privacy and space for the staff? Is the lighting good?

These few questions should help you to look at a building more critically. Taking photographs will also help to concentrate your attention on important and interesting aspects of the building. An even more useful exercise is to do some sketching—you don't need to be an expert. The aim is not to produce highly finished drawings but to train yourself to look more closely at buildings.

Studying architecture

Of course, your observations of buildings will be helped if you do some background reading on the subject, too. A list of some good books on architecture is given on page 47; and you will find many more in a library with a good arts section. To keep up with new developments in architecture, you need to read trade magazines.

You can also learn about contemporary architecture by following the architectural reporting in a good newspaper. Here, you can find out about important exhibitions on architecture, too. Lectures and walking tours devoted to architecture may be advertised in local papers or on a school or library bulletin board.

To become a fully qualified architect requires a long training, usually a minimum of seven years. If the prospect of seven years of intensive studying and internship seems too burdensome, remember that there are a number of other careers associated with architecture. Interior designers often work closely with architects in planning public buildings. Architectural firms use the services of skilled draftsmen, secretaries, and other administrative staff. And if you are interested in constructing buildings, then working in the construction field is an obvious choice.

On the other hand, you may prefer to study the history of architecture with a view toward teaching or writing about the subject. Some universities offer degrees in architectural history. If you would like more information you should talk to your guidance counselor.

Plans and elevations

Books on architecture will almost always contain plans and elevations of buildings. These are precise scale drawings. A plan, also called a ground plan, show the structure of a building as though a horizontal slice has been taken through it. An elevation shows a head-on view of the exterior. These illustrations (left) show the main floor plan and front elevation of Chiswick House, in London, which was designed by its owner, Lord Burlington, in the early eighteenth century. A great admirer of Palladio, Burlington modeled his house on the Italian master's Villa Rotonda. The plan is almost exactly symmetrical.

Chiswick House

Glossary

Aesthetic (adjective) Relating to the sense of the beautiful; artistic. (noun) The set of principles underlying a particular style—for example, the functional aesthetic.

Aisle Part of a church, or other building, which is separated from the main area by a row of columns or piers, for example. In a church the aisles run down either side of the nave.

Ambulatory An aisle that encloses an apse.

Amphitheater A circular space surrounded by rising tiers of seats built by the Greeks and Romans—the Colosseum in Rome, for example.

Apse The curved end of a church, behind the main altar, or containing it.

Art Deco A style of architecture and design popular in the United States and Europe in the 1920s and 1930s.

Articulated (as an architectural term) Given clarity, emphasis, or visual interest by means of one or more architectural features, such as windows, moldings, or pilasters.

Ashlar Masonry composed of smooth, rectangular, closely fitting stone blocks.

Asymmetrical Having different elements on either side of a central dividing line.

Avant-garde Describes pioneers in the arts, whose ideas are in advance of those currently accepted.

Batter The sloping face of a wall.

Battlement The fortified top of a castle wall.

Buttress A brick or masonry support for a wall to counteract the outward thrust of a roof or vault.

Calligraphy Artistic script produced with a brush or pen.

Cantilever A horizontal projection, such as a step or balcony, that has no external braces but is supported by a downward force behind a fulcrum (the point on which a level turns).

Centrally planned Describes a building that is designed around one central point.

Clerestory The upper part of the wall of a church, above the aisles, usually with windows.

Cloister An enclosed, covered walkway surrounding a courtyard in a monastery or convent.

Coffered Describes a carved or molded ceiling with recessed squares or many-sided shapes.

Colonnade A row of evenly spaced columns.

Cosmos The concept of a structured universe.

Coving The concave molding at the point where the ceiling joins the wall.

Crenellations The alternate indentations of a battlement.

Crossing The point where the transepts cross the nave in a church.

Entablature In Classical architecture, the decorated horizontal beam supported by columns.

Façade The face, or elevation of a building, usually referring to the front of the building.

Figurative A term used in painting or sculpture to describe images depicting figures as distinct from abstract images.

Functionalist Relating to the belief that the form of an object or building should be determined by its use.

Half-timbering A method of building in which the walls consist of an interlocking timber frame. The spaces between the timbers are filled with wooden laths covered in plaster.

Icon An image, usually painted or carved in relief, that is sometimes the focus of devotions in Orthodox Christianity.

Incised Cut or engraved.

Masonry Construction in stone.

Mausoleum A large tomb.

Molding A form of decorative woodwork or plasterwork.

Monumentality The quality of being impressive and imposing like a monument.

Mosaic A type of floor or wall decoration formed of small pieces of colored glass or stone, called tesserae, set in cement.

Motif A theme taking the form of a piece of decoration on a building; a curling plant motif, for example, would be found in Art Nouveau decoration.

Nave The main part of the interior of a church that is flanked by the aisles.

Oculus A circular opening in a wall or in the top of a dome.

Order A type of column and entablature forming a style, e.g., Doric, Ionic, Corinthian.

Pavilion A building joined to a main building at the end of a wing.

Pediment A triangular or semicircular projecting feature crowning a door, window, or portico.
Piazza An Italian word for a large, open space in a town.
Pier A stone pillar supporting an arch or vault.
Pilaster A rectangular column that projects only very slightly from a wall. In Classical architecture it would be in the form of one of the orders.
Pinnacle A small, decorative spire, used in Gothic architecture.
Portico In Classical architecture, a partly enclosed space at the front of a temple or house, at the center of the façade, and composed of columns and a roof.
Post-and-lintel A method of construction consisting of columns with a horizontal beam laid across their tops.
Prefabricated Made of sections constructed separately then assembled on the site.
Prestressed concrete A development of reinforced concrete in which the steel rods are replaced by wire cables in ducts.
Reinforced concrete Concrete in which steel rods or mesh is embedded to increase its strength.
Ribs The structural bands in a ceiling vault.
Rusticated Applied to masonry in which the edges of the stone are beveled and the face of each block is roughened.
Sensuous Appealing to the senses.
Stylobate The platform structure on which a colonnade stands.
Symmetrical Having all elements identical and in balance on either side of a central dividing line.
Tracery Narrow, decorative stone carving separating the panels of a Gothic stained glass window, or forming a screen, or applied to a wall.
Transepts The two arms of a cross-shaped church at right angles to the nave and chancel.
Travertine A cream-colored porous limestone.
Vault An arched ceiling or roof of stone or brick. A barrel vault is the simplest of vaults, being like a continuous arch.

Further Reading

American Architecture Now, by BARBARALEE DIAMONSTEIN (Rizzoli, 1985).
The Architecture of Europe, by DOREEN YARWOOD (Chancellor Press, 1974).
The Churches of Rome, by ROLOFF BENY & PETER GUNN (Weidenfeld and Nicolson, 1981).
A History of Architecture, by SPIRO KOSTOF (Oxford University Press, 1985).
The Horizon Book of Great Cathedrals, by EDITORS OF HORIZON MAGAZINE (American Heritage Publishing Co., Inc./Bonanza Books, 1984).
The Indian Style, by RAYMOND HEAD (University of Chicago Press, 1986).
Living Architecture, Chinese, by MICHELLE PIRAZZOLI-T'SERSTEZENS (Grosset & Dunlap, 1971).
A Pictorial History of Architecture in America, by G. E. KIDDER SMITH (American Heritage Publishing Co., Inc., 1976).
Pride of Place, by ROBERT A.M. STERN (Houghton Mifflin, 1986).
Primitive Architecture, by ENRICO GUIDONI (Harry N. Abrams, Inc., 1978).

Index

Numbers in **bold** refer to illustrations.

Adam, Robert 31
Adler and Sullivan **35**
Alberti, Leon Battista 24
Art Deco style 38, **39**, 41, 45
Art Nouveau style 36

Babylonian architecture 9
Baroque style 28, **29**, 30–31, **30**
Barry, Sir Charles 34
Bauhaus 37, 39
Bernini, Gianlorenzo **5**, 28
Borromini, Francesco 28
Bramante, Donato 24, **24**, 26
Brunelleschi, Filippo **23**, 24
Byzantine architecture 13–14

Canada
    Habitat, Montreal 40
castles **18**, 18–19
cathedrals 6, 18, **21**, 22–23, **23**
China
    Temple of Heaven, Beijing **16**
Chinese architecture 16–17, **16**, 24
churches 18, 20–21, 27, 34
Classical style 11, **24**, 26, **27**, 28, 31
Colonial style 32

De Stijl movement 37

Egyptian architecture 9, **10**, 11
England
    Blenheim Palace, Oxfordshire 31
    Brighton Pavilion, Sussex 33, **33**
    Castle Howard, Yorkshire **30**, 31
    Covent Garden, London 27
    Crystal Palace, London 35
    Houses of Parliament, London 34
    King's College Chapel, Cambridge **6**
    Lloyds Bank Building, London 41
    Rochester Castle, Kent **18**
    Royal Crescent, Bath **32**
    St. Bride's Church, London 31
    St. Pancras Hotel, London 34, **34**
    St. Paul's Cathedral, London 31
    St. Paul's Church, Covent Garden, London 27

Flamboyant style 22
France
    Bibliothèque Ste. Geneviève, Paris 35
    Chartres Cathedral 22
    Château de Chenonceau **26**
    Eiffel Tower, Paris 35
    Notre Dame, Paris **21**
    Notre-Dame-du-Haut, Ronchamp **38**, 40
    Palace of Versailles 28, 31, **31**
    Paris Opèra 35
    Place des Vosges, Paris 27
    Pompidou Center, Paris 40, **41**
    Reims Cathedral, **22**
    St. Denis, near Paris 22
    Ste. Madeleine, Vézelay **19**
    Unité d'Habitation, Marseilles 38
    Villa Savoye, Poissy **37**
Functionalism 37, 38, 45

Gabriel, Ange-Jacques 31
Garnier, Jean-Louis Charles 35
Gaudí, Antonio 36, **36**
Georgian style 32
Germany
    Altes Museum, Berlin 32
    Bauhaus, Dessau 37
    Burg Stahleck, Bacharach 18
    Residenz, Würzburg 30
    Rhine castles 18, **18**
    Staatsgalerie, Stuttgart 41, **41**
    Vierzehnheiligen 30, **30**
Gothic Revival 33, 34–35, **34**
Gothic style 6, 22
Graves, Michael 41
Greece
    Parthenon, Athens **10**, 11–12
Greek architecture 11, 24
Greek Revival 32–33
Gropius, Walter 37, 39

Holland 37
    Amsterdam **8**

Inca architecture 17
India
    Taj Mahal, Agra 15, **15**
    Viceroy's House, New Delhi 38, **39**
International style 37
Iran
    Mosque of Masjid-i-Shah, Isfahan **14**
Islamic architecture **13**, 14–15, **14**
Italy
    Ca d'Oro, Venice **21**
    Colosseum, Rome 12
    Florence Cathedral 23, **23**
    Pantheon, Rome 12, **12**
    Pazzi Chapel, Florence **23**
    Il Redentore, Venice 27
    San Giorgio Maggiore, Venice 27, **27**
    Sant' Andrea, Mantua 24
    St. Peter's, Rome 24, 26
    St. Peter's Square, Rome 5, **5**
    Sta. Croce, Florence 24
    Tempietto, Rome 24, **24**
    Villa Rotonda, Vicenza 27

Japanese architecture 17, **17**
Jefferson, Thomas 32
Johnson, Philip **6**, 38, 41
Jones, Inigo 27

Kampuchea (Cambodia)
    temple at Angkor Wat 16, **16**

Labrouste, Henri 35
Le Corbusier **37, 38**, 38, 40
Lutyens, Sir Edwin 38

Mackintosh, Charles Rennie 36
Mesopotamia
    Hanging Gardens of Babylon 9
    Tower of Babel 9
Mexico
    Castillo of Kukulcan **17**
    Mexico City 17
Michelangelo Buonarroti 26, 28
Mies van der Rohe, Ludwig **6**, 37, 38, 39
Modernist style 37–39, 40–41
Mondrian, Piet 37

Nash, John 33, **33**
Neoclassical style 31–33, **31**, 41
Neumann, Balthasar 30

Palladio, Andrea 26–27, 28, 31
Perpendicular style **6**, 22
Peru
    fortress of Sacsahuamán 17
    Machu Picchu ruins 17
Piano, Renzo 41
Postmodernism 41
Pugin, Augustus Welby Northmore 34
pyramids 5, 9, **9**

Renaissance 23
Rococo style 30
Rogers, Richard 40–41

Roman architecture 11, 12, 24
Romanesque style 18, 20–21, 23
Russia 14

Saarinen, Eero 40, **40**
Safdie, Moshe 40
Schinkel, Karl Friedrich 32
Scotland
    Edinburgh New Town 31–32
Scott, Sir George Gilbert **34**
Second Empire style 35
skyscrapers 35, 36, 38, 41
Spain
    Casa Milá, Barcelona **36**
    Church of the Sagrada Familia, Barcelona 36
Stirling, James 41
Sullivan, Louis Henry 36
Sydney Opera House 40

Tiepolo, Giambattista 30
Turkey
    St. Sophia, Constantinople **13**, 14

United States 33, 35, 39
    AT&T Building, New York 41
    Boston 27, 32
    Chrysler Building, New York 38, **39**
    Dulles Airport, Virginia 40, **41**
    Executive Office Building, Washington, D.C. 35
    Falling Water, Bear Run, Pennsylvania 40, **40**
    Guaranty Building, New York 35
    King's Chapel Boston, 27
    Philadelphia 32
    Portland (Oregon) Public Services Building 41
    Prairie Houses, Chicago 39
    Seagram Building, New York **6**, 38
    St. Patrick's Cathedral, New York 34, **34**
    State Capitol, Richmond, Virginia 32
    TWA Terminal, Kennedy Airport 40
    Williamsburg, Virginia 32
Utzon, Jørn 40

Van Alen, William 38
Vanbrugh, Sir John **30**, 31
Vitruvius 44

Welsh castles 18
Wood, John, the Younger 32
Wren, Sir Christopher 30, **31**
Wright, Frank Lloyd 39–40, **40**

Picture Acknowledgments

Richard Bryant/Arcaid 40 (top), 41 (bottom); James Austin 38; BBC Hulton Picture Library 39 (left); J. Allan Cash 4: J.H. Cordingley 30 (top); David Cumming 36; Angelo Hornak 7 (inset), 39 (right), 40 (bottom); British Architectural Library/RIBA 44; Ronald Sheridan 7, 9, 12, 15, 16 (bottom), 17 (top), 18 (left), 19, 21 (inset), 21, 22, 24 (bottom), 25, 26, 30 (bottom), 31 (bottom), 32, 34 (bottom); Wim Swaan 14; Topham Picture Library 31 (top), 34 (top), 35; ZEFA 5, 8, 10, 13, 16 (top), 17 (bottom), 18 (right), 23, 27, 29, 33, 41 (top), cover. The artwork on pages 11, 20 and 2 is by Jenny Hughes.